My Expressions of Love for You

Upon a Moonlight
Kiss

For information, write
Sayspire Media,
615 North Bush Street, #831,
Santa Ana, CA 92702.
www.Sayspirequotes.com

ISBN 978-0-9858951-5-0 (hardcover)
978-0-9858951-3-6 (paperback)

Written by Joshua Cintron and Priscilla Zamora

Cover art by Melinda De Ross
(https://www.coveredbymelinda.com)

To: _____

From: _____

Date: _____

When I was a young man,
I dreamt of many things:

success, popularity, money.

But,

those dreams pale in comparison to you, a
beautiful red rose

in the garden of my life.

If asked to describe you by friend or foe, my
smile would gleam and expose

the off-color white of my teeth when I speak
your name. My eyes, widening

with fervor, pressing to exalt your love.
I would silence the logic

rushing to save me from sharing
these emotions. I would share,
then re-share, the

greatness that you are.

A memory of you popped into my head today.
It brought

a calm, soothing presence, the type I feel when
our bodies

labor in the exhale of our breath, cooling the
passion in the room.

It is a wonderful feeling, knowing memories
such as these come to mind when I least expect
them,

when I need them most.

When you look at me, your stare penetrates
me. A cool breeze triggers

a synchronized dance of goosebumps taking
stage on my arms.

Quick is the cadence, twitching my limbs,
chilling my body in excitement.

Have you ever thought, you were born for me?
I was born for you?

I have.

I sit, close my eyes and a vision of you dancing
comes to mind. You *twirl*

gracefully; hand on the edge of your dress,
head tilted back, eyes closed

to the place, filling you with joy. You are
captivated by the music,

setting you free from the worries and
distractions of life. It is a fantastic image

my mind settles on.

In the minutes after we met, we silently
questioned ourselves

that we found our partner in life. Shortly
thereafter, our question was answered,

a becoming that neither you or I expected. This,
what we have, became

a love many search the ends of the world but
seldom find. To think –

to know, you and I share a love like this, is
beyond any poetry I can create,

felt only when our bodies are next to one
another.

I search for eloquent words to describe my feelings for you.

Futile are the attempts because only my heart will ever know.

You complete me.

You make whole what was empty, the inner most parts of me.

You make me feel wanted, desired, appreciated. I guess

whatever eloquence I searched for is plainly explained by this, I love you.

At times, I feel as though our love is challenged by friends, colleagues,

family and those jealous of what we have. I see it. They tell us.

Let us continue this ride of love
we share together, for as long

as it should last – beyond time and space that has no end.

I often tilt my head up to the skies,
point my finger to the boundless space

of dark matter smashing together to form the
beauty, the intelligence of

this existence and thank the powers that be for
creating you.

In you, I see myself alive. In you,
I see a beautiful future unfold.

In you, I see the definition of love
that the dictionary doesn't have.

In you, I see life – life
for so much more.

When two people click as you and I did, it is a
moment of surreal joy - a

cosmic event beholden to nature, orchestrated
by powers far greater

than you and me. All we can do is embrace
what we have, like children

embracing a teddy bear at night, and hold
close the night we shared beneath

the lights of our grand city,
when our lives become complete.

To kiss her, the one who embodies, sensuality,
intelligence, wit, beauty,

is to see the impossible become possible. Such
grace, levitating

across his heart. Surreal to know,
he is me, she is you.

When the light leaves my room and my head
falls onto the white, linen

pillow, I see only the vision of you. What
darkness prevails, should not

blind the image of your smile that brightens
my eyes. Shutting them only

brings you closer – allowing me to rest from the
day but not of the serene

presence of your face.

I recall the moment when we looked into each other's eyes, and a truth

revealed itself. Light illuminated your skin, radiating your eyes

in openness, touching my body in weakness. My hand reached

your cheek, grazing the smoothness of your skin, stopping time in its tracks.

We stood there, hostages to the silence of one another, embracing

the beautiful romance that we still share this day.

I've heard people say love doesn't exist, but I've learned those

people say it because they've yet to experience love for themselves. I've

heard people say love is a fairytale found in children's books, but I've

learned those people say it because they've yet to experience love to write

their own book. I was one of those people and what you've done to

change my mind, to make me a believer in the fairytale of love, is a

story I share with you now—to the rest of the world, for all of time.

Baby, what are you doing to me? At breakfast, lunch, and dinner, the

thought of you consumes me. I cannot escape your voice nor the image

of your face. You overtake every process in my mind, leaving behind your sweet

kiss. How I long to be next to you, every second of the day.

The tender kiss of your lips is potpourri of love in the house

of my heart.

I met you with the strength of a newborn, who's
path was lost,

where the desire of physical touch and empty
hearts from many was sought.

I am as a lucky child with loving parents for
this fate that leads me

to you.

In the clouds that form in the blueness of day, I
see not the shape of an animal

or a familiar object but that of your face. It
absolves whatever troubles

I'm dealing with. I cannot escape the thought of
you; you are everywhere

I am to be.

I look at your beautiful face. How lucky I am to have a woman like you.

Such natural beauty derails me. What positive vibes comfort me. I pinch

myself, talk to myself, try to make sense of what you do to me,

but there is no logic or reasoning to explain it. I'm just lucky I get to call you mine.

We are a magnetic field attracting one another.
Despite the distance

separating us or an object getting in our way,
we will come back

into each other's arms forever more.

You are mine to have and hold, to love and support, to caress and kiss, to hug

and comfort. Ever so often, to take on doubts, to wallow in pity, to conquer

fears, to dry pain-filled tears, to ensure a meaningful life filled with love,

secured by nature's perfect symmetry and timing.

As daylight falls unto the moon's shadow, I lay
to rest and pine for your

touch. I dine in sleep with memories of us
intertwined, for you are my one

true love.

You rest there, I rest here. I cannot touch you or
wrap my arm around

your body or kiss your neck. You are there, I am
here. I close my eyes and

wonder if you think of me. Torture lives here
now, as we are apart. Your

touch is quiet, it caresses my name. I shall
close my eyes, litter my dream

with memory of you.

Our love is far beyond the moment we first met,
strengthened in the times

we hold hands, walking the halls to dinner,
sharing in drink and song.

Should difficulties find us like rain after a
tornado, may we weather such

storms with the raincoat of our love's bond.

It took a lifetime, my lifetime,
to find you. You honor me. My soul

smiles; I met my match. Lucky in this lifetime,
grateful as I am to bask

in the glory of a woman like you.

When your lips meet mine,
an electrical current of ecstasy
travels throughout my body,
stimulating oxygen that warms
my hands,
charges my heart,
fills my soul with life.

When we sit on the couch and your head rests
on my chest, the warmth of
your body surrounds me
like a wildfire.
The scent of your freshly
bathed hair
fills the room in
beautiful incents.
In the rhythmic beats
of my heart,
your head
rises and falls,
and the lids to my eyes
slowly descend into a
deep sleep.

I love you.
Do you hear it?
Do you feel it?
Does your heart sense it?
Does your mind receive it?
I say this unto you,
like water nourishes
a bed of flowers,
this is my love for you,
giving of everything
to your heart's hand.

Dedication.
Commitment.
Trust.
Honesty.

You hold these attributes
in the palms of your hands.

You expect only the same in return
that I hold them in my hands.

With clinched fist; open hand; wave of a
finger, they combat the howling wind of
temptation blowing in and around life.

No challenge will ever be too great, to give
unto you what you give unto me
a dedicated heart, a committed mind, a
trusting mouth, and an honest love.

When a destination is on your mind and you're
determined to get there, I sit back and watch
you gather your things: a purse, car keys. You
catch me

watching you, but I play it off as if I'm
searching for something near you. You
continue preparing

for your exit from our home, leaning on the wall
with one hand, purse

on your forearm of your other, shuffling
sandals onto your feet. You're ready.

You glance at me, seeing if I notice you leaving.
I do and a smile as wide

as an ocean shore, eyes twinkling like a bright
star in the night, accompany

the kisses traveling upon your hands toward
me, wishing me goodbye.

This night, you are gone from the bed we make
passionate love on. The spot

where you lay; cool and untouched like the soil
unearthed when a rock

is turned over. Though I slide my socked feet
under the colored sheets,

under the floral-patterned comforter, I can find
no heat, no comfort,

the furnace of your body is gone from this bed.

If I could sing the song of love you now read, a terracotta-lined street

leading to you would be my stage. I would hold Spanish guitar

under stars in a black sky with tightly strung cords to carry unto you,

the undistorted tone of my love. I would set my eyes upon the balcony

where you sit, press my lips, open my heart, pour unto you music your soul

can dance to. I would lift you with a voice to be heard in a language only

we understand. I would sing to you the joy and happiness filling me

with song. I would sing to you, oh, I would sing to you, my love.

I am not the one who chooses to watch a
romantic movie, cuddling on the sofa

with a blanket in each other's arms, you are. I
am thankful,

thankful for you showing me not with words but
in actions, how to enjoy

small seemingly insignificant moments.
Though the audio

from the movie spreads throughout the room
we're in, my body is calm,

my mind is content in the normalness you
cared enough to show me.

I love how your ears remain deaf
to the paparazzi of family who spread news,

good or bad, of the happiness we share. We
            can speculate

how our names pass through the editorial halls
of family members, deciding what

should be broadcasted to the public of gossip.
            Regardless of what airs, you

are the calm of a lake, motionless,
            unwavering in the story of us.

Sometimes it feels like I walked through a stargate created by other worldly beings, hidden

from humanity somewhere deep in the Earth's core, to a dimension of time, past or present, to meet you.

I call you my girl, the one who will dine, the
    one who will laugh,

the one who will fight, the one who will
encourage, the one who will give,

the one who will lay down, the one who will
hold, the one who will live,

the one who will love, in the palace of my soul's
kingdom.

I tell you I love you.
You respond, "I love you more."
I reply, "No, I love you more." You retort, "No, I love you more." With a smirk, and a half smile, I reply, "Uh, no. I doubt that, because I love you more."

You continue, end the discussion by kissing me on the lips.

We play this song and dance almost daily, trying to convince the other that our love is greater. It's cute how you won't lay down and accept that I love

you more. I hope this book expresses the immense love I have for you because there isn't a rebuttal in the world that can top that.

Some work tirelessly for recognition, money or promotion. They give of their free time, time away from those they love. I can never be that person because being with you is

greater than any monetary reward. Sipping

coffee late night, watching silly shows, laughing, smiling, that's my reward, seeing you hold me, kissing me as we fall asleep.

I stood next to you, leaning over the roof's edge. I was hesitant to look at you, not because you were a woman draped in intellect and beauty, but

because I was afraid of falling in love.

I stared intently at the neighborly buildings shading us from the moons light. I finally built the courage to look at you - to look at you like an

alien appearing before a sceptic -

you did the same. In the nanoseconds of our eyes meeting in the vastness of space, my lips clamored to touch yours; my hands ached to interlock

with your perfectly manicured hands. I drowned in the hazel ocean of your presence.

My love, a White South Sea pearl
desired by men and women
for centuries, elegant beyond all others,
the most valuable
there could be, you are.

I walked on a sidewalk the other day; noticed
colorful flowers without a name. My nose

recalled the fragrance they emitted.

I stopped.

Closed my eyes. Breathed in the pleasant
perfume swirling around me,

perfume that brought the memory

of your smiling face,
to my peaceful mind.

I want to let you in on a little secret about the pleasure of your voice. When you speak, it's with the comforting softness of a white goose down pillow. When you're stressed or worried, your words drip through the filter

of logic, delivering goodness. When you're excited, your words shower those who are present with adoration, celebrating the joy emanating from within you. And, when you press your chest against my back, lift both of

your arms under my armpits, guiding your hands to my shoulders for rest, your whispers in my ears are a lullaby, putting whatever chaos that finds me, to sleep.

There is a romantic picture of us sitting

at a candlelit table, enjoying dinner,

in the shadow box picture frame of my heart

it hangs on a rod of blood traveling about

my body. It is an image that will remain

with me until this life of mine is no more.

I want to be happy, happy in love, in work,
because that's how I envision

life should be. I may strike out on the work
part but I keep going up to the

batter's box, swinging away, knowing my hit,
my time will come.

One thing I'm certain about, falling in love
with you is a grand slam

to be celebrated, to be read for generations
to come.

I may not express my feelings about anything to you very often. I may rely on logic too much which gives the impression that I don't care. I may

do things that make you question

if I do, in fact, love you, but truth be told, I love you. I really, really love you. You take the best of me which may not be much at times and make it better.

My life is beautiful with you in it,

guiding, mentoring and showing me what true love really is.

I can't give you the life you deserve, right
now, and it frustrates me. You may tell me
everything is perfect, you don't need anything

else, but I want to give you everything you
never had: a place to call your own, the car of
your dreams, relief from bills and debt, and

a platter of travel destinations to choose from.
I want to give you all these things in a future
where you and I can enjoy the fruits

of our labor, and ride off into a never-ending
sunset the rest of our living days.

Guys I've talked to, who are in relationships
seldom say, "I can't wait to get home, so I can
spend time with my girl!"

Sad.

Here I am, looking at the clock hanging on the
white walls in my office, wondering how much
longer I have before I can gather my things
and race home to you.

En route, I think about what we'll eat for dinner,
what show we'll watch on TV or where we will
make love this time around.

Isn't it validating to know our relationship is
one we both genuinely want to be in, and not a
hindrance that keeps us apart?

Our love is an hourglass of sand. When you
are down, sand filling my bulb

empties into yours. When I am down, sand
filling your bulb empties into

mine. Should we remain together, nothing,
not even time,
can stop
our love.

The door knob rattles; the deadbolt turns;
muffled sounds of bags shuffle in the distance;
rings and keys wrestle with one another;
weather stripping, sealing the entrances

to unseen inhabitants slightly pops like bubble
gum bubbles, welcoming home the queen of
this castle, you.

Many look upon you with great desire, with
lustful intentions. I know because I see
them as you parade in front of me.

With the effort of walking to and fro,
you exude appeal,

as a charlatan casting spells upon the eyes
gazing from them who know not why they stop
in their tracks, mesmerized by you.

These elbows, carved of granite, covered in
      flesh, sit atop tables,

providing the stand to a pedestal of palms that
      hold my ragged face. A statue

of David cast in love, I become set forever
      in the direction of you.

One in 13,983,816:

the odds of winning the lottery;
the odds of winning you.

Oh, French kiss, oh, French kiss, where art
thou French kiss? Such romanticism are words
creating the play of lips, guiding the prop

of tongues past the white porcelain
gates, into the moist pastures of a
scene. How I long for us to be the
thespians to such a play.

Uncover the blanket from your bare feet, feel the
        coolness of my kiss,

the breeze of my breath leaving my nostrils
        comes to penetrate the warmth

of your toes, to deliver my adoration
unto you.

Who else is there for you but me?
Who else is there for me but you?

You and me, me and you. That's it.

When I haven't seen you the entire, day, I am the son running to his parents, stretching out his arms, readying for an embrace of uninhibited love.

Each morning, my peacefulness of sleep,
     you by my side is dissolved

by the aggravating melody of the alarm. How
     the dark, silent room filled

with the coldness of morning is. The spot
     where I lay, a heated indent rising

like cake batter in an oven, furnaced by your
     warmth, all disrupted

by the obligation of work. I long to spoon you
     once again.

Run your freshly manicured French tips on the inside of my arm; start at

my elbow, down my forearm to the tip of my finger. Repeat nine more times.

Watch my body turn into jello by the slightest touch.

I come into your life to add, to bring joy
and excitement, to bear the burden of your
stressors, to be the reason why

you should leave work and come home.

If I become a bag of rocks weighing you down,
I'll cast myself into the ocean, freeing you to
love another.

I turn the chrome knobs in the shower, more
hot than cold, wait several minutes for the
bathroom to fill with steam. A couple more
minutes, to drown the light, to let the moisture
gather on the mirror above the sink.

The steam-filled condition forms droplets
of sweat near the temples on each side of
my face. *Ready.* I press my damp index finger
against the moist mirror, writing,
"I love you."

Emotion of love, water contained in a fire
hydrant of my soul, released by

the firefighter, the hero, you, is a geyser of
words, sprouting for all to see.

This relationship we share, harmonious,
jubilant; the wedded bliss of bells ringing

from the mountaintop, overlooking the sky's
beauty of our future, picture of perfection.

Loveliness you are, the showy blooms of a
lily, vibrantly colored

in red, orange, pink, and white, planted on a
mid-summer's day in a garden.

We look at each other frequently.
I am enthralled

in your evenly separated eyelashes fluttering
in the foreground of your eyes

like butterfly wings in midflight.

The treehouse I built in my heart to
share with another laid desolate in the passing
years, vanished, forgotten.

The dusty sheet of memory covering
the vision of such a place, welcoming two
children, giddy in love, removed itself when you
appeared.

Who am I to question the bright light,
traveling from beyond the reach of
understanding, across the vastness of
space and time, past other habitable
places that comes to me in the
form of you?

Oh, how I long to see you in a tight, fitted dress painting your curves, high heels lifting you above the crowd;

natural makeup showcasing your flawless skin.

Doused in perfume of sweet elegance, you set ablaze desire within me, quenchable by your touch.

Come here, bring me into you. Wrap
your arms around me; hug me.
Let the peaceful quietness surrounding
us, say what you or I could never
adequately express in words.

Wrinkles on my face tell all
I've gained in this life
I live.

Handsome only
to you, conversely, your face is
preserved in youth, without
wrinkle, like the bouquet of roses I
send you on a romantic occasion.

Anyone setting their sights on you
is awed
by your sheer beauty.

Straddle me, oh, wait. I mean, sit on my lap, grab me with both your hands, stare into my eyes, tell me you love me.

Kiss me.

Turn my head, kiss my neck, blow on the spots still moist from your kiss with your warm breath. Nibble on my ear lobe. Lick it. Run your tongue up and down like you would ice cream dripping over the side of a cone.

Don't stop. Keep going.

Do you feel that? My heart racing, pounding against your chest, my body yearning for more?

When people express feelings
for the person they love,
some tattoo a name
on their body;
others scribe initials
on the trunk
of a tree
or in newly poured concrete.
I choose ... no,
I etch your name
on the walls
of my unconscious
and conscious mind,
where no matter the day
or time, in this life
or the next, the memory
of you is the very fiber
of me.

If I could kiss you right now, I would. Not the
quick-peck-on-the-lips kind either,
but the deep, passionate, soul-shattering kind
where your eyes glue shut and heat
begins to rise-up your back. When
     you emerge from the psychedelic
     feeling, you're speechless, hostage to
     the euphoria of love's kiss.

I am enamored with you, a child brimming with excitement. Yes, I am a child and

from time to time you may tell me so, but I am alive, happy, excited for life

because I am in love. There's no greater feeling than to give love and be loved.

You are the cause, the reason why I put hand
to pen, pen to paper, pouring

words from the well of passion as the
love-struck fool I am.

As a child, I didn't know what a musical instrument was. As a teenager, I could care less about the musicality of singers. The naivety in my youth slowed me

to the splendor of music, the romanticism of a melody filling the soul with gladness. As grey begins to line the edges of my forehead, I have become a lyricist, playing the harmony

of your body, the tone of passion in your heart, the music your soul loves to dance to.

Hundreds, if not thousands, educated, trained
masters of metaphors and similes,
are true poets.

I'm not.

I'm just a man, expressing an immense love to a
woman who captures his heart.

Give me your lips
and the wetness
of your kiss.

I'll give you
the electricity
of our chemistry.

You never ask for candlelight dinners, heart-shaped chocolate boxes, long-stem roses, or opulent jewelry, though you deserve all of them on a nightly basis. I may not give

these things, and I may often fail you

but know that I muster the strength within me to make sure you are loved, cherished, respected, treated as my equal, to convey to you, you are number one in my heart my one and only.

Always.

Without you
in my life.
I am a tree
without water,
brittle branches
broken to the touch,
leaves as fried chips,
rotting roots
fertilizing the soil
for some other tree
to grow.

You are the masterpiece of
nature's artistry, I am the museum chosen to

curate such priceless art.

www.ingramcontent.com/pod-product-compliance
Lightning Source LLC
Chambersburg PA
CBHW071848090426
42811CB00004B/528